GRIT
AND
GUMPTION
A COWGIRL'S GUIDE

GLADIOLA MONTANA

GIBBS · SMITH
P
PUBLISHER

SALT LAKE CITY

12 11 10 09 08   10 9 8 7 6 5

Copyright © 1999 Gladiola Montana

Published by
Gibbs Smith, Publisher
P.O. Box 667
Layton, Utah 84041
Orders: (800) 748-5439
www.gibbs-smith.com
Illustrations on pp. 12, 34, 36 by L. Bark'karie
ISBN 0-87905-916-8

Printed in China

Some
men can't be trusted
too far—
others can't be trusted
too near.

A

wedding ring

is a one-man band.

Occasional
flashes of silence
can sometimes be mistaken
for brilliance.

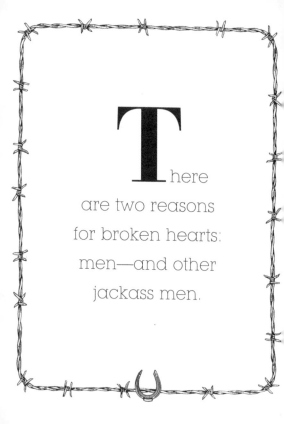

There are two reasons for broken hearts: men—and other jackass men.

The
cure for most
cases of
"love at first sight"
is a second look.

When

you start walkin' on air,

be sure that you're not

hangin' yourself.

With

a man,

trust is a must.

Your jeans are too tight when you gotta plan ahead to sit down.

Good
gals wear white—or any
other color
they darn well please.

Courage
and guts
make your word good.

Try
to live till you die,
not just till you
get run over.

It's easy
to know somethin' is wrong,
not so easy to know
what to do about it.

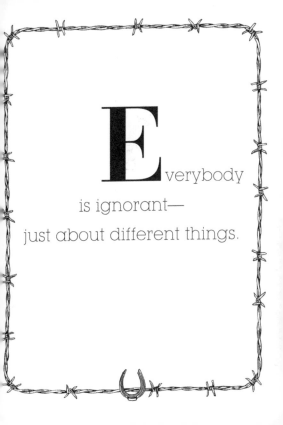

Everybody
is ignorant—
just about different things.

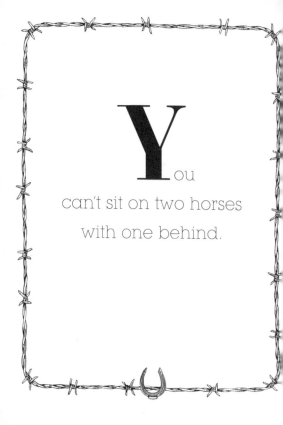

You
can't sit on two horses
with one behind.

The warmest fire comes from wood you chop yourself.

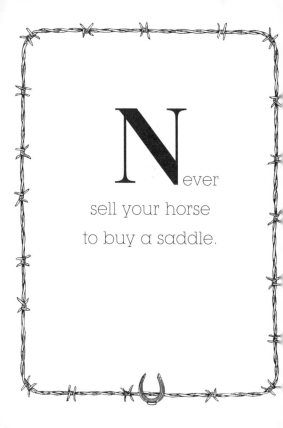

Never
sell your horse
to buy a saddle.

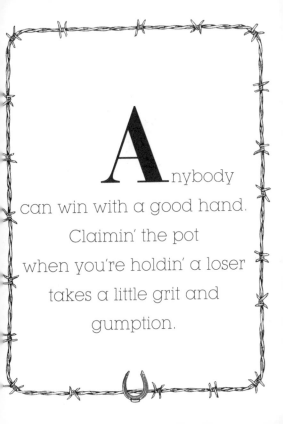

Anybody can win with a good hand. Claimin' the pot when you're holdin' a loser takes a little grit and gumption.

Not
makin' a choice
is makin' a choice.

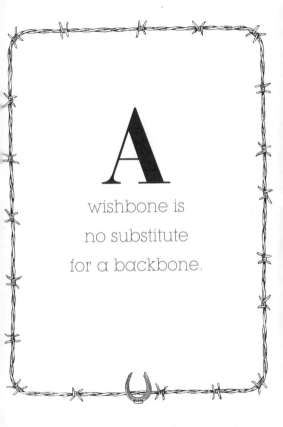

A

wishbone is
no substitute
for a backbone.

Important

comes in two sizes:

yours and mine.

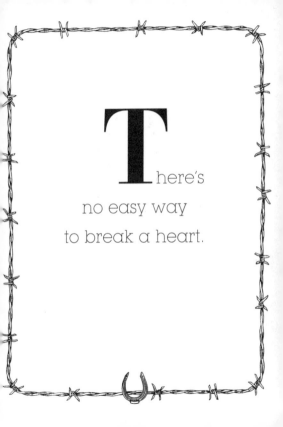

There's
no easy way
to break a heart.

Don't
pack a piece
for bluff
or balance.

Another word for mistakes is "experience."

A

sharp eye is worth
more than a wink
from Lady Luck.

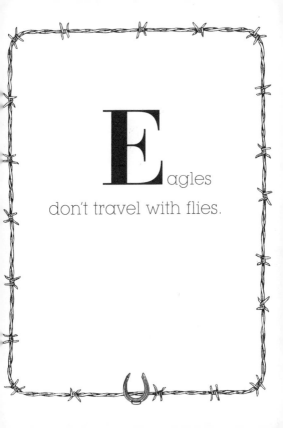

Eagles

don't travel with flies.

The
problem with dishonest jerks
is that they think
everybody else is
just like them.

I
f
you think about it,
girls do have more fun.

A
cackling hen
is either laying
or lying.

A

taker hates to give.

If
you're in love, you only
have yourself to blame
and everybody else has
you to blame too.

Just
because a man is polite
don't mean he ain't a
lowdown skunk.

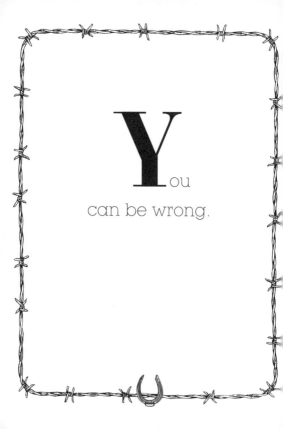

You
can be wrong.

A

loose horse
is always lookin'
for greener pastures.

The
size of his hat
is no measure of a man.

A

lack of tact
is as bad as
a lack of virtue.

Ridin'
backwards
gets you nowhere.

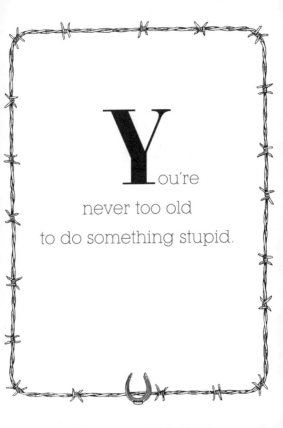

You're
never too old
to do something stupid.

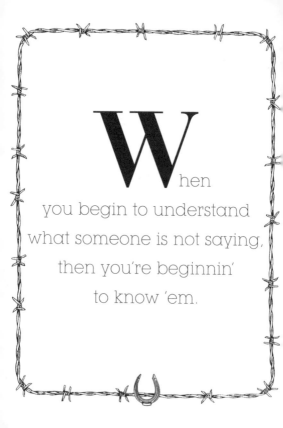

When
you begin to understand
what someone is not saying,
then you're beginnin'
to know 'em.

Men
are from Mars,
and some of 'em
from even farther out
than that.

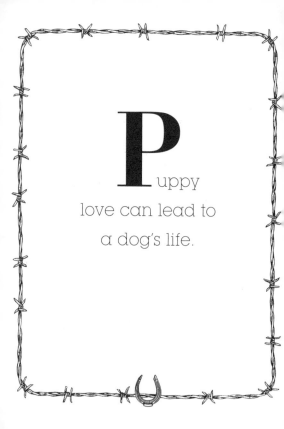

Puppy
love can lead to
a dog's life.

Strength
comes from wrestling
with our weaknesses.

What
you can't push
you can usually pull.

*F*or *example* is not proof of anything.

There
is no such thing
as hair too big.

Patience.

Better
to make a man
out of a fool
than a fool
out of a man.

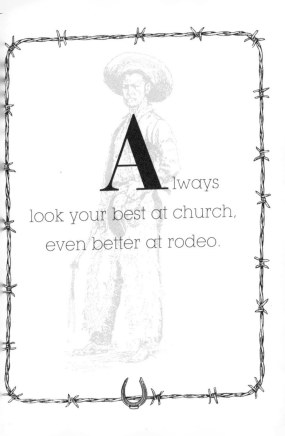

Always
look your best at church,
even better at rodeo.

A

good friend

is a second self.

Life
is too short
to be little.

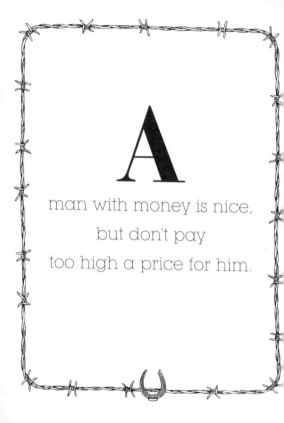

A

man with money is nice,
but don't pay
too high a price for him.

God
forgives . . .
that's his business.

A pig is a pig
even if it can
do tricks.

It
may be that
barking dogs don't bite,
but *they* don't know it.

What somebody says about you tells more about them than you.

Never
love a man
you don't like.

The
best cure for a pain
in the butt
is to kiss him good-bye.

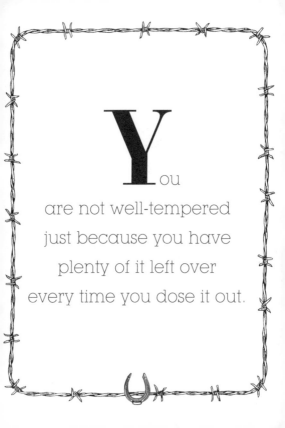

You
are not well-tempered
just because you have
plenty of it left over
every time you dose it out.

Love
is the whoopee cushion
of the heart.

Love
is a gamble, not an
insurance policy.

Miracles
come from heaven,
but only after you
work like hell.

It
may be more romantic
to be the first love,
but it's better to be the last.

When
a man asks a woman to
share his lot,
she has a right to know
how big it is.